MW00953988

לאגנ

REDEEMED

לאגנ

REDEEMED

PASTOR ROGER FORD

authorHOUSE®

AuthorHouse™
1663 Liberty Drive
Bloomington, IN 47403
www.authorhouse.com
Phone: 1-800-839-8640

© 2012 by Pastor Roger Ford. All rights reserved.

No part of this book may be reproduced, stored in a retrieval system, or transmitted by any means without the written permission of the author.

Published by AuthorHouse   08/31/2012

ISBN: 978-1-4772-6677-9 (sc)
ISBN: 978-1-4772-6676-2 (hc)
ISBN: 978-1-4772-6678-6 (e)

Library of Congress Control Number: 2012916275

Any people depicted in stock imagery provided by Thinkstock are models, and such images are being used for illustrative purposes only.
Certain stock imagery © Thinkstock.

Because of the dynamic nature of the Internet, any web addresses or links contained in this book may have changed since publication and may no longer be valid. The views expressed in this work are solely those of the author and do not necessarily reflect the views of the publisher, and the publisher hereby disclaims any responsibility for them.

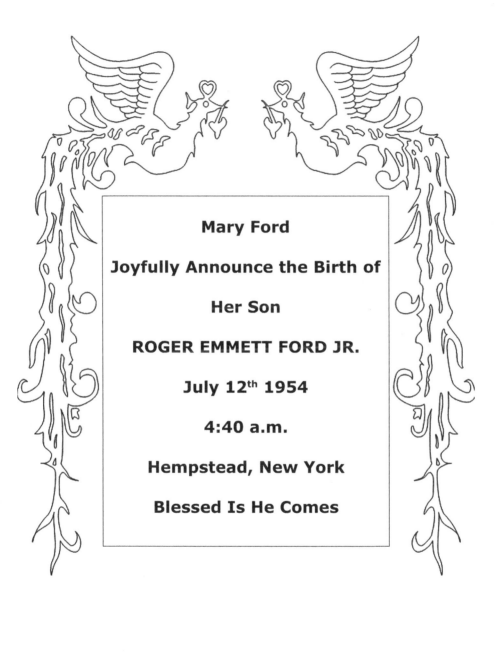

Mary Ford

Joyfully Announce the Birth of

Her Son

ROGER EMMETT FORD JR.

July 12th 1954

4:40 a.m.

Hempstead, New York

Blessed Is He Comes

Dedication

Who can find a virtuous woman? For her price is far above rubies. The heart of her husband doth safely trust in her so that he shall have no need of spoil. She will do him good and not evil all the days of her life. Proverbs 31:10-12

This book is dedicated to my loving wife, Pastor Karen Ford, a Godly woman who believes in the Word of God. She has uncompromising faith that God IS, and will deliver, heal and set free those who ask.

When I surrendered my life to the Lord, I found the true meaning of unconditional love. I saw her relationship with Jesus Christ rise up and outward towards me. This love allowed me to become the husband and Godly man that is required by the Father and our Savior.

I love her for all that she is and all that she has experienced. I would not take back one day of our years together. She is the one that convinced me that it is okay to be an imperfect human being. I know in her eyes I am perfection and in the eyes of Jesus.

Thank you for loving me.

I love you always . . . .
Pastor Roger Ford

A Prelude To A Kiss

Several years ago I thought I was in a comfortable place in my healing. My deliverance however; was not complete. There was bondage that I chose to remain in. Areas of my life that I subconsciously **refused** to surrender to God. The opposite of freedom is slavery. I chose to remain enslaved to people, places and things from my past.

God predestined my coming into relationship with Apostle Shawnette A. Houghton, Presiding Prelate-LFC-Apostolic Ecumenical Community Network of Kingdom Churches & Ministries. A global network in Chicago IL. How can I thank you enough? I love you. Thank you for showing me what freedom looks like. You realized there was yet sexual and relational healing and deliverance to be done. You not only expected, but demanded that we walk in the calling that God has ordained in our lives. You are a Powerful, Anointed woman of God. You walk in the Word, and you chastise with a two edged sword. Thank you for removing my grave clothes. Thank you for your support and for instilling greater courage to expose the enemy and live victoriously. Thank you for receiving me just where I was supposed to be, for releasing and ordaining me to do that which God has called me to do. As you continue to release, and preach the Gospel, may others be healed as they are touched by your shadow when you pass by.

Your Devoted Servant
Pastor Roger Ford

Foreword

I believe that an individual can abstain for years and not be delivered; likewise one can be delivered yet not healed; while most will settle for being healed while never being made whole.

In the midst of the rubble of sexual and relational idolatry and underneath the dust of ashes of perversion and brokenness, a leader emerges whose transparency in the truth about his struggle transforms. Psalms 51:8 speaks of the rejoicing that can come forth from the broken. Rarely in the lives of broken people do you hear the sounds of repentances that reverberate as rejoicing.

Well the Blood speaks and testifies as it has washed clean the stain and stench of sin.

Up out of an open grave comes forth a Pastor Roger whose life boldly testifies to the title of his book Redeemed. The bible says let the Redeemed of the Lord say so. Pastor Roger speaks. He has a passion for seeing souls saved and set free. Holiness is what he lives for. His praise is personal, for it is his bones telling his redemption story. Earlier I stated that few live whole. Pastor Roger is an example of being Delivered! Healed! and made Whole!

God has a way of allowing the paths of destiny to cross. Eight or nine years ago Pastor Roger and I met, and I had the pleasure of meeting the testimony of deliverances housed in Pastor Roger. Since then I have had the honor of watching God complete a work.

It is not his story that will captivate you because everyone has a story but it is the power of God in his process, the Blood Jesus paid for the plan for his life and the Holy Spirit relentless pursuit to keep what was predestined.

As you journey through the pages of his life may you be introduced to **Pallet** (GOD of deliverance).

Thank you for coming forth and allowing me to be one of those who unwrapped you. May My Ceiling Be Your Floor.

Humbly Submitted,

Apostle Shawnette A. Houghton, D.P.TH
Presiding Prelate
LFC-Apostolic Ecumenical Community Network of Kingdom Churches & Ministries

Acknowledgments

With the deepest gratitude I wish to give thanks to each person who have inspired, encouraged and demonstrated steadfast belief in my transformation and the call of God on my life. Thank you for sharing your knowledge and wisdom regarding walking in the faith and service.

A special thank you to Apostle John Carter, Sr. Pastor of Praise In the Earth Institute. Your faith in me did not go unnoticed. Thank you for confirming the Pastoral Mantle upon my life, and watching as Jehovah prepared me to go into the enemy's camp with my testimony to release those in captivity to sin's grip. You decreed that I must preach Truth wherever I journey in my future. I hope you find that I have kept my word.

Bishop Ray Llarena of Harvest Christian Center in Chicago IL. You were the first positive male role model and the first to speak greatness in my life. You spoke with excitement and great expectation and gave me permission to move forward in God and be free. (Young man God has great things for you). Thank you for new beginnings.

Pastor Richard and Dr. Naomi Roberson set very high standards in ministry. Open doors for outreach ministry and insisted the work is not inside the church. What would Jesus do? Jesus would be outside the church amongst the people. Thank you for your insight, guidance and biblical knowledge.

Prologue

Several books have been published recently regarding Gods miraculous deliverance of the homosexual. We are in a season when we have finally removed Jehovah Elyon from the invisible box the body of believers had placed Him in and rendered Him powerless to take on the sin of homosexuality. God's power is limitless and well able to perform His promises*. **It is our faith in His power** . . . . **and our belief in Him as** . . . . **God** . . . . **that falls short**.

We believe that by the spoken **Word, He** created the heavens and the earth. We believe the **Word** healed the sick, raised the dead, open the eyes of the blind and cast out demons. We believe that the wind and the waves obeyed the **Word**, and yet we can't phantom that **at the Name of Jesus,** the spirit of homosexuality must bow, obey the word and flee . . . we do not believe that.

This is not a blueprint on how to transform your life and live as a heterosexual. It is not about marrying the right gender or having acceptable sex with the right person. This message is about the transformation into becoming the Godly man or woman that our Father (God) would be pleased with through His Word. We must understand that our lives are not our own. Our souls belong to Him. A God that is greater than ourselves. He made us in His image, which is perfection. Psalm 139:14 "I will praise thee; for I am fearfully and wonderfully made". Does that mean that because I have feminine characteristics as a man, or masculinity as a woman, that I am not fearfully and wonderfully made? Who said that my soft and gentle ways are not the characteristics of God? Why can I not love a man or is it the way that I love that man that God is displeased? Which is it that God would want me to change, my character or my behavior? My behavior would demonstrate my sinful nature, but my softness and gentleness; (my character) would demonstrate my humility and love for God.

Homosexuality is an abomination before the Lord. Let us be clear about this Truth. It stinks in the nostrils of God. He abhors such sexual immorality and perversion because it is sinful. If a man lies with another man as he lies with a woman, both of them have committed an abomination. They shall surely be put to death. Their blood shall be upon them. (NKJ,

Leviticus 20:13) but the bible also emphasizes"I beseech YE therefore brethren, by the mercies of God, that you present your bodies a living sacrifice, holy, and acceptable to God, which is your reasonable service, and be not conformed to this world; but be ye transformed by the renewing of your mind, that you may prove what is that good, and perfect will of God. (Romans 12:1-2)

I am a Breathing Witness that God can/will and is still well able to deliver the Homosexual. And because so few believe that our God is all Powerful, that our lives are predestined, mapped out and planned, I share my testimony of Deliverance. It is not a "Once Upon A Time" event, but a lifestyle that will overwhelm you with the need to change . . . the question is, will change ever come? But the Word . . . . God's Word . . . promised me that He who began a G-O-O-D work in me is faithful to complete it.

I share my life story not because the previous authors have failed to give an accurate account of their Sodom and Gomorrah experience, but because of HIM (GOD) I have overcame him (satan) . . . by the Blood of the Lamb and the Word of my testimony. God's Word confirms this. Herein is my journey in the raw. It is hard Truth. It bears witness to the undeniable power of a Triune God to transform even the chief of sinners. I pray that when you complete this message you will understand that **God loves the sinner but not the sin.** I pray that your ears will hear the voice of God and that your heart will receive His Son Jesus the Christ, Our Lord and Savior. May the Holy Spirit direct you towards the Light.

Pastor Roger E Ford Jr.

Chapter I

Westbury, New York, a quaint, quiet setting . . . with secrets. It housed "ungodly" spirits that rampaged through the community. Overly populated with religious institutions and mad houses, these spirits freely masqueraded themselves amongst the young people. Lust, perversion, deviant sexual appetites were all closeted and unspoken behaviors. But there still remained those who had a desire to serve God. In the face of adversity, they instilled in us to live by faith and stand on God's promises. Faith pleases God; it motivates us and gives us the unction to press towards the mark of the high calling of God in Christ Jesus. Phil 3:14. HIS purpose . . . . HIS plan for our lives.

Life was a joy playing in the streets with childish euphoria. We were a family of five, three siblings, my mother and I. We had an absentee father, he was considered m.i.a. A shy kid, somewhat introverted, I was rejected by most of my peers in school because of my inadequate social skills. Musical instruments gave me purpose. First the piano next, the violin. I was trying to embrace myself and find out what would hold my interest.

My feminine tendencies were obvious and noticeable by those who had influence in my life. Un-be-knowing to me they were depositing seeds in my mental. Satan was working with the Spirit of Rejection. The seed took root when I was denied my first blessing and heritage, my father's name . . . . when a choir director, (I was six years old) determined that singing was not my calling and asked my mother never to bring me to choir rehearsal again. The enemy was always there, prepared to kill and destroy my spirit. It is evident how the prince of darkness was fertilizing the ground for the lifestyle of homosexuality through my insecurities. He whispered in the ears of those available to him and revealed to them my dominant feminine attributes. I would hear insensitive comments about the way that I walked the sound of my voice and my body gestures. I was no longer referred to as a sissy. They called me

F A G G O T . . . .

I later learned how dehumanizing that term was. **"Satan has desired to have you and sift you as wheat, but I have prayed for you that your faith**

should not fail, and when you have returned to ME, strengthens your brethren". Luke 22:31-32.

During this season I was not actively involved in any homosexual behavior. I didn't know what homosexuality was . . . . I didn't know who I was. Who am I? Am I who they say that I am?" This journey from the pits of hell to the introduction into the Light and Life of my Savior Jesus Christ has been a painful one. It has harbored anger, frustration, unforgiveness and insecurity, even into my manhood. It brought with it fear, disease, and drug addiction.

It . . . *this thing* . . . turned my natural love for a woman into lust for a man. I *willingly* allowed these men to use my body for their own lustful satisfaction. Willingly . . . . , we must accept accountability for our actions on this journey.

Can one be born into homosexuality? YES . . . Now that I have your attention, allow me to clarify this statement. In Psalms 51 David understood that he was a transgressor, he had iniquities and he needed to be cleansed from his sin. He understood "why" he was the way that he was. Verse 5 confirms "Behold, I was shapen in iniquity; and in sin did my mother conceive me." Christ gave us instructions on how to change. But I believe you are born into homosexuality because we are born into sin. We MUST be born again. Jesus told Nicodemus "Verily verily I say unto thee, Except a man be born again, he cannot see the kingdom of God." John 3:3 Paul said "for the invisible things of Him (God) from the creation of the world are clearly seen, being understood by the things that are made, even His eternal power and Godhead; so that they (mankind) are without excuse. There is no excuse for mankind living a sinful life. Can we not sit at the cross and be saved? Is this grace not extended to everyone, yea . . . . even the homosexual is heir to His Grace.

Conversion . . . ***(Introduction)*** I believe that one can experience the stages of pregnancy from the spirit realm of darkness as a result of negative seed planting. Those ungodly seeds are deposited in your spirit from childhood until one day a lustful spirit (man or woman) coaches your delivery into existence . . . . when false love is introduced to you. He has various ways of manipulating you.

We, the rejected, the outcast, consume our immediate surroundings with the stench of our needs. The stench attracts familiar spirits. My natural need for masculine mentorship was twisted into an unnatural relationship when a man sniffed my need for acceptance and told me how beautiful I was. It was the deceiver there waiting to receive me at the birth canal opening. The deceiver waiting . . . convincing me that it was acceptable and natural for a man to touch and penetrate me as a man penetrates a woman. He kissed me, held me and made me feel secure in my

4

skin. His intention was to use me to satisfy the lust of his flesh. The end result, confusion and shame that would hinder my destiny, causing me to doubt who God said I am.

The act dehumanized my manhood and caused a downward, spiraling effect into the beds of other men. The pain it caused was the beginning of the dissension of my life into darkness. Even with my conversion into this lifestyle, my sexual role was chosen for me. "Faithful are the wounds of a friend, but the kisses of the enemy are deceitful". Proverbs 27:6.

Chapter II

We were, as a family, baptized in Jesus Name at the Church of The Lord Jesus Christ. God inspired me to introduce my family to Christ, although my knowledge of him was limited. Baptism meant spiritual renewal, sin-less. I left it all in the liquid grave. What I did not realize at that moment was that I had shifted from the natural realm into the spiritual realm. A **spiritual battle** was in full force.

The Lord had given me a natural appetite for the female persuasion. I was very attracted to and curious about girls. The enemy; however, whispered lies and spread deceit about my sexual preference and eliminated any chance of my dating girls.

I have always felt a personal connection with the Lord, a Love for Him and a Fear of Him. Even in my blackest nights, I was confident that He was there but

Satan had another plan. He introduced new friends to me. These friends and I attended church together and as they called on the Name of Jesus, they took me deeper and deeper into darkness.

Even every one that is called by my Name: for I have created him for my glory, I have formed him; yea, I have made him. Isaiah 43:7

Enter . . . my birth father **(not my biological father)**, but he whom introduced me to a sexual and sinful behavior. He displayed so much interest in me. Immediately I was invited to his house. He had something he wanted to show me. ***Did I know what he wanted to show me??? YES***!! Did I know the full scope of his intention? Absolutely not! I had a need to feel loved. He led me into a bedroom in a dark basement and assured me what he was about to do would not hurt. "Lie face down" he said, and I could feel his overpowering presence covering my body as he tried to penetrate me. The pain was unbearable. Fear gripped me! I asked if I could leave and the answer was a resounding "NO". I indicated I had to use the restroom. I jolted up the stairs through the living room, past his mother and out the door. Change had taken place. Confusion . . . . humiliation . . . and the shame! I really believed I was a faggot. The words of his mouth were smoother than butter, but war was in his heart; his words were softer than oil, yet were they drawn swords. Psalms 55:21. But it was thou a man mine equal, my guide and mine acquaintance Psalms 55:13

Birth father +Introduction = Choice. I knew it was sinful. I knew it was not the right choice to make! Why did I feel so worth-less, so de-humanized that I would willingly accept a man's invitation into a dark basement and allow him to treat me as a female? Why would I allow a man to empty himself into my body? Was it the names/labels that were already rooted in my mind? Sissy, faggot, or the insensitive seeds deposited in my spirit? "You are never going to be worth anything"! "You walk and act like a girl". What I did not realize was THAT "one moment", THAT "one incident" would impact my life in a way that would change my destiny and it was not for good. Depression, drug addiction, sexual addition, pain, bad relationships and thoughts of suicide.

No longer a rumor, all the young boys got wind of my homosexual experience and it had a domino effect. We were ignorant to the depth of SIN we were committing. But we KNEW it was sinful. We determined that it was only sex, but . . . we were aware that there was something soulfully wrong with what we were doing.

After a few sexual experiences I had become adept at getting the attention I needed. In school life was a living hell. The boys loved me by night and enjoyed taunting me by day. My grades faltered. There were times I intentionally manipulated others sexually. Someone else needed to share this burden, this curse that seemed to have me in a cocoon. Westbury was a Sodom & Gomorrah experience in itself. Most young boys were involved in homosexual behavior before they ever approached me. Some are married today, other have died while struggling with their demons.

When I ponder on it, I believe even in the darkness that awaited me in the basement, God had a plan for me. His plan was and is to use me as a canvas and paint a picture of a *redeemed homosexual.* To show His Glory to those whom deemed it impossible to restore a homosexual. The Bible repeatedly confesses that He set the captives free. "And that they may recover themselves out of the snares of the devil, who are taken captive by him at his will (II Timothy 2:26)

The enemy's desire was to overtake me psychologically, spiritually and physically. He is the master deceiver. He would twist an innocent situation into a perverted one. My mind takes me back to my early years when there was a young boy with beautiful green eyes. I was so amazed with him because I had never seen an African American with green eyes. I begin to think that I was born gay because I had mistaken amazement for attraction.

In retrospect, it was just his green eyes. The enemy deceived me. I was too young to understand what masculinity or femininity was. I did; however, understand and appreciate beauty and I found his eyes beautiful. I also found feminine apparel and characteristics beautiful. I didn't know what to do with these feelings. There was no one to share these feelings with. So I called on the name of the Lord. I prayed for opportunity to come into the fullness of God's glory in my life. My growth was stunted by the enemy. "But know that the Lord hath set him apart that is Godly for Himself: the Lord will hear when I call unto Him". Psalms 4:3.

Chapter III

I returned to church, struggling with my sexual identity. I volunteered to assist the Pastor cleaning the church once a week. *I knew he recognized the spirit upon me*. Did he respond in the manner a Shepherd should when he recognizes the enemy ready to sift his sheep? Did he question me about my feelings, fears or even my fantasies? Did he pray for me, or cover me under the Blood for refuge from the enemy's intentions? The Pastor did, what so many Shepherds do, denied what the Lord has exposed to him. Maybe if he denies the truth, it will go away or we will outgrow it.

On Sunday morning the Pastor had a guest seated on the pulpit. He announced that he was in the process of ordaining this young man. My immediate thoughts were "I volunteer to clean the church every Saturday, why was this young man getting the Pastor's attention? Immediately following service, I befriended this young man. I asked if he wanted to hang out with me? We ended up in a hotel room.

I was surprised there was NO hesitation from him! I had recognized the spirit this young man was operating in? He recognized the feminency in me. His masculinity deceived the Pastor, and he did not recognize the spirit of homosexuality upon this young man. This spirit is so deceptive that we only recognize the feminine male. We conclude that two feminine males are attracted to one another and this constitutes the homosexual. There is a masculine role in this scenario, but we fail to acknowledge this role. We don't look for this in the equation, and so we are deceived.

After returning to church the shame of his actions weighed heavy upon him while he sat on the pulpit. Witchcraft, deceitfulness, and manipulation are all characteristics of the spirit of homosexuality. From this point forward I knew how to use the power of darkness to manipulate, deceive and provoke other young men, married or otherwise, and I did . . . I manipulated with vengeance. In whose eyes a vile person is contemned; but he honoureth them that fear the Lord. He that sweareth to his own hurt and changeth not. Psalm 15:4

When you walk in darkness, you are unaware of what is coming towards you. In the darkness we stumble and we brace ourselves for the fall. We may attempt to break the fall, but the fall is inevitable. There we find our weakness in the flesh and the condition of our hearts. It is deceitfully wicked. There stands the strong-hold embedded in our spirit that will not allow us to be released from the desires of our flesh. *It is then that we realize our sin override our relationship with our Savior Jesus Christ and the salvation that He has offered to us.*

We continue to walk through a spiritual grave yard reading the tombstones with names of people, places and things that put us in this situation. My soul would struggle and linger in the valley of indecisiveness, which cause the delay of my resurrection from death to life. Ephesians 2:4-5, But God, who is rich in mercy, for His great love where-with he loved us, even when we were dead in sins hath quickened us together with Christ, (by grace ye are saved).

I believe that how we are introduced to sex, our first impression of intercourse have a great impact on our attitude towards sex. If rape or crisis proved to be our introduction to sex, sex can become powerful at one end of the spectrum, or traumatic and disgusting at the other end of the spectrum with no happy median. When I so easily seduced that young man, the question is what had occurred in his life that made him so willing to partake in an unnatural act from the pulpit? What made him feel it was okay to follow a stranger to a hotel room.? The heart is deceitful above all things and desperately wicked; who can know it? Jer. 17:9

Chapter IV

It was my first year of high school. As with any alma mater, the initiation was to beat up the arriving freshmen Thank God I had someone who knew me and had fore-warned everyone not to touch me. My god-sister, Marie. For the first few days my immediate concern was passing the boys locker room and bathroom. Schoolmates were threatening to take me into the restrooms and cause me bodily harm. That also meant that I could not use them. The rumor that I was "gay" was true and unlike today, gay was not an acceptable lifestyle on the streets of New York City. It was very difficult to concentrate in class.

After school one day a classmate asked me to hang out with him. His father owned a cab stand. This was not our first sexual encounter together. I was to meet him at his father's cab stand to indulge in a lil sexual activity. When I arrived there it was just he and I; however, to my surprise, two others arrived.

These were known as the three bullies in the community. The three towered over me in weight and height. All three proceeded to rape me. I was warned what would happen if I told anyone. Raped by three young men. We demonstrate compassion, understanding and sympathy when a woman is violated. But when a man is violated, especially if he is known to be in a particular lifestyle, there is no display of compassion. Some find it amusing. After one finished with me, another would come. When it was over, I left and went home alone, humiliated, confused, and consumed with shame. I felt deceived, used and betrayed, and I wanted to know why?

The enemy, being the deceiver that he is, convinced me of how powerful I was because I was able to sexually satisfy three boys. As if I had conquered some great feat! They bragged about it amongst themselves. In their small minds I was some type of trophy. Three sick, sex craved boys, assaulting another. In my mind I was thinking they obviously liked me. One of them had the audacity to approach me several times after that. The other two never approached me again. *Then when lust hath conceived, it bringeth forth sin: and sin, when it is finished, bringeth forth death. James 1:15.*

Lust (the evil one) deceived all of us into partaking in that which is an abomination in the eyes of God. Myself, because I entered into an agreement to have sex with a male, the others for the rape that occurred. This was the starting line of my decline towards my finish line, which would have been an early death, had I not been born again!

When I decided to disclose to my mother how I felt about my sexual identity and my preference in a life partner, her reaction was explosive to say the least. I was still faithful in attending church, and it was important that I tell her personally. I didn't want her to hear about it from anyone else. I sat at the table and I blurted out "Mom I am Gay'! Her reaction . . . you are what???? You are gay??? You are a faggot????" She went into total shock. No, you can't be!! The only way she knew to respond was "I am going to call your Pastor".

The church was the important entity in our family. Using me as a vessel to introduce my family to the church and knowledge of the Savior was a part of God's plan for my life. Confessing homosexuality during that era was God's greatest sin. You were, without a doubt on the road to hell and damnation to burn in fire and brimstone. Satan was turning the coals just for me. But I needed compassion and acceptance. I was so confused with these feelings and I didn't know what to do with them. I wanted answers, not hysteria, drama and rejection. *I was screaming in the spiritual realm, PLEASE QUESTION ME!!!!!! . . . what . . . how . . . who and why do you feel that you are gay?* Her response made me feel ashamed and rejected . . . . again.

The Pastor wanted to speak with me; I thought to chastise me *privately*. I was waiting for him to call me into his office. That never happened. During the service my Pastor boldly announced to the congregation that a mother had called him, very distort, crying and advised him that her son was a faggot. My disclosure became the sermon for the evening. "Turn your bibles to Genesis 19th chapter." You knew what was coming!

He repeated the story of the doomed homosexuals in the city of Sodom and Gomorrah, and how God destroyed the city because of the homosexuality that existed there and how the men of the city lusted for the angels sent by God. The truth is God destroyed the city because He couldn't find one righteous individual in the city. *Hopeless and defeated, I never returned to that church again.* Rebellion reared its ugly head and attached itself to me. I am what I am . . . . **Proverbs 23:7: For as a man thinketh in his heart so he is**. My heart was no longer with God.

Roger Ford and Mary (mother) Ford

Chapter V

**Deliver me O Lord from the evil man:
preserve me from the violent man
Psalm 40:1**

I delve into the homosexual lifestyle and met other people with identity issues as mine own. I visited gay clubs. I no longer cared what people thought or about my family because they too were living in shame. This rebellious spirit caused me to plunge deeper in sin . . . sex and drugs.

At sixteen I had my first long term relationship with an older man. It lasted two years, but the abuse lasted a lifetime. I often feared for my life. There were episodes when I had to lock myself in a closet for my own safety. This spirit was a stalker, an abuser, a pedophile with a lust demon. He enjoyed forcing me to perform sexual acts. He reeked of lust and perversion. It did not matter when or where we had sex. He tickled my ears and promised gifts, etc. False love, false security, walking in narcissism and pride. There is always a price to pay.

My sinful nature had no barriers. I did not discriminate when it came to pleasing my flesh. A young Bishop was running a revival in my hometown. It took him seven days to seduce me. Little did he know I was willing and waiting to be seduced. Beware of false prophets, which come to you in sheep's' clothing, but inwardly they are raving wolves. Matt 7:15.

"Can I drive you home after service Brotha Roger?" I knew in my heart what he wanted but I played it off. While driving me home, he stopped the car and told me that he liked me. We played that game back and forth for a minute and then he kissed me. It was not enough that I had ended a physically abusive relationship. I allowed myself to become immediately entangled in a mentally abusive one. With a man of the Clergy at that! God Forbid! I was desperate for love. His power and his authority allowed me to feel good about myself.

There was never any sex involved in our relationship, just kissing, fondling and body language. This freed him up emotionally from thinking that he was a homosexual and that he had not involved himself in any type of homosexual act. THE DEVIL IS A LIAR. It is not that these men are not chosen by God, but that they are disobedient to the Word of God and unfaithful. "For there shall arise false Christs and false prophets and shall shew great signs and wonders; insomuch that, if it were possible, they shall deceive the very elect." Matthew 24:24

Heterosexual men only want to experience the sex act because it is a sinful act . . . a forbidden act. And when we are forbidden to do something, it becomes more desirable, more enticing. The euphoria is not getting caught and then we want to hide under the shame of it. It is the original sin . . . . Disobedience. And the Lord God called unto ADAM and said unto him, where art thou? Only through God's Word do we realize the depths of our disobedience. Then we question God and ask why?

With disobedience come shame, fear and guilt. God has greater things for those who accept responsibility for their behavior. Forgiveness, healing and His great love for His creation. God has always given us a way of escape. No temptation has overtaken you except such as is common to man; but God *is* faithful, who will not allow you to be tempted beyond what you are able, but with the temptation will also make the way of escape, that you may be able to bear *it.* 1Corithians 10:13

The men I really found interesting were the so-called Bi-Sexual men. What does that mean? When one is sleeping with a person of the same sex, it is a homosexual act. When one sleeps with a person of the opposite sex, it is a heterosexual act. Homosexual does not define who you are, it is what you do. It is an act, a behavior.

The Bi-Sexual are those who visit the bath houses and drive around all night looking for young boys to fulfill their lustful fantasies. Some even dress them up in women panties, wigs and lipsticks to deceive themselves into thinking they are not really performing a homosexual act. The bible says that we deceive ourselves and change the truth into a lie. These men then return home into their beds with their wives and girlfriends. These are the ones who wear the business suits, the construction hats and the pastoral robes. The ones who claim homophobia and cast shame upon those in the lifestyle. They bring gifts of HIV/AIDs, herpes, and STD's home to their wives. Then they are ashamed because they hate what they are and what they do.

They see themselves as God sees them, sinful and broken. James 1:8, a double minded man is unstable in all his ways. A Bi-Sexual man can never live a stable life. He is unstable in his sexuality, his marriage, his beliefs and his relationship with God. He is uncertain of what he wants and who he is as a man. Then we cry out to God for help. Well, help is on the way. This is why God made a sexual relationship between a man and a woman and placed the sexual organs to the front of the temple (the body). So while making love, you can look into one another's eyes and see their soul and say "I love you". The bone of my bone and the flesh of my flesh and they become one.

This is the true representation of marriage from creation. A certificate was never given to Adam and Eve. It was the sexual connection that ordained the marriage. Marriage is honorable in all and the marriage bed is undefiled. But whoremongers and adulterers God will judge. Vows are exchanged during the marriage ceremony, either biblical or personal. These vows are made before and with God and He receives and accepts them. Adams vow to Eve is Genesis 2:23 and 24 "and Adam said to Eve "this is now bone of my bone and flesh of my flesh, she shall be called "woman" because she was taken out of man." Therefore shall a man leave his father and his mother and shall cleave unto his wife and they shall become one flesh.

Not only did God establish a covenant between them but he also commanded his creation (man and woman) to reproduce as part of their vows. This is why God made marriage between one man and one woman. There shall be no whore of the daughter of Israel, nor a sodomite of the sons of Israel. Thou shalt not bring the hire of a whore at the price of a dog into the house of the Lord Thy God for any vow: for even both these are abominations unto the Lord thy God.

27

Deuteronomy 23:17-18. Marriage cannot and will never be acceptable to God between the same sexes.

Whenever I had a relationship with a Bi-Sexual partner, it was an overwhelming feeling of conquest. He had lied about who he was. I had conquered a real 100% man. One who didn't sleep with other men. It gave me confidence to know that I had that kind of power. I knew who I was when I got out of bed. However; he did not want to accept who he was and the act that he had just performed with another man. As always, after the act, there was a withdrawal. The shame and guilt had overridden the excitement of the sexual act we had just committed. Then . . . he thinks of his wife. This is why God calls the homosexual a covenant breaker, fornicator and unrighteous. My sin had consumed me.

Chapter VI

For all that is in the world, the lust of
the flesh and the lust of the eyes
and the pride of life is not of the
Father, but is of the world".
I John 2:16

I moved forward and began dating other people. One evening I decided to visit a disco called **Better Days** in New York City. The atmosphere was charged with excitement. The dance floor was very dark with a glimmer of light. Out of the darkness, this tall, fine dark man appeared. Call it a "Billy Dee" moment. It was the deceiver at his best! He was vain, self centered, and a momma's boy. This was the beginning of a thirteen year relationship that ended in tragedy and triumph! Tragedy because he died, triumph because I came to know the MORE of Jesus Christ. It did not matter the infidelity, the lies, the deceit and betrayal. My plan was to stay in this relationship if it killed me, and it almost did. Know that in this lifestyle, faithfulness is insignificant. If you were considered "eye candy", you had a one way ticket to perversion. The spirit of Pride had invaded my spirit. "That about sums up the homosexual lifestyle.

After a very bad disagreement, I decided to leave and visit a friend. When I arrived at the friend's house, three men were standing behind me in the hallway. They asked me if I was looking for the same person. I responded "yes." A moment passed and no one answered the bell. As I began to walk away, I saw a silver flash in my side, and one of the men said "get in the car". I obeyed, overwhelmed with fear. I had no idea what they wanted and I did not have any money on me. We were sitting in the back seat of the car with one of the man on each side of me. We drove into a park that is well known for Gay Cruising called Prospect Park.

They told me to get out and all four of us proceeded further and further into the park. I was fearful, because it was known that many bodies had been found in this park before. They told me to take my clothes off, and I began to slowly remove my clothing. I knew they were about to kill me or run a train on me. I could see they had intentions of taking my clothing and making me run through the park naked. Fear ran through me, and I had to think quickly how to get out of this situation, so I confused them. I started yelling as loud as I could "ARE WE GOING TO DO THIS OR WHAT?? Two of them started laughing while one of them raped me and the other two walked away.

I was thankful to God that I was still alive because it could have turned out quite differently. I was very angry. This was the fourth time I had been raped. Once, in a men's rooming house that I resided in while my apartment was being refurbished, a man followed me into my room and forced me on the bed. At that moment I was hoping that he did not look up and see that I had 500.00 in the light fixture. I was so accustomed to being raped that it seemed like a normal occurrence. I expected it to happen. My spirit was opened to all types of sexual experiences. I began to feel that sex was a way to punish myself.

After the rape my life seemed painful, unrewarding and meaningless. Most men in the lifestyle were violated in some way. Men violate men, just as they violate women. Society focuses on a man's physical and decide it is impossible for a man to rape another man. It does happen and it happens often. Returning home, I never mentioned the rape to my lover. Your question is why? Some things you decide to struggle with silently. The relationship was riddled with lies and infidelity. Would it have mattered that some stranger raped me? What would have been his response? I did not want to know.

Spiritually I felt like I was receiving a warning from God that I needed to change my life. GOD was not pleased. There was a moment when an overwhelming spirit of fear came over me. It was as if Death was chasing me! I desperately needed to find a church. I walked all around my community searching for a church on a Friday night. The Baptist church was closed. The Methodist church was closed. I walked down a hill and I saw a storefront church and it looked as if it was closed as well. There were no windows in front, but it had a huge cross lit up on top of the church. As I was about to turn around and go home, I heard music and singing from inside. I walked up to the front door and the Ushers tried to lead me to the front. I refused and sat in the back. I felt like a sinner that needed to be forgiven . . . . A fearful sinner that needed to come to repentance. When the Pastor, Elder Wills, called an altar call, I slowly got out of my seat and went to receive prayer. I could feel the love of Christ and the love of the Saints filled the room.

I returned home excited . . . ready to start my new Christian life. I had been forgiven . . . . I knew I had been forgiven . . . . I wanted him to know that I had really given my life to Jesus and I began to witness to him. Now that the Holy Spirit had shown me what I was really doing, I thought that if I helped him to accept Jesus Christ as Lord and Savior, he would not go out to look for another relationship. I wanted Jesus and him too!!!! Notice my selfish motive for witnessing to him? The bible clearly states that homosexuality is an abomination before the Lord. But I wanted God and I wanted my lifestyle too.

He came to church and sang in the choir, participated in bible study and Sunday morning service. If God loved me as much as He said He does, then He will wink His eye at my lil sin as long as I worship Him in spirit and in truth and continue to shout over my unholy stuff! God had another plan. I was faithful in my prayer life, as Choir Director and Vice President of the Usher Board. Save, Sanctified . . . . and filled with His precious Holy Ghost, speaking in tongues as the spirit gave me utterance . . . but I was keeping my eyes on him. My tongues were speaking one thing, but my heart was being deceitful. I needed deliverance from myself. Then I received a message from the Lord. "I am God! And before me there is no other".

The knowledge that I had to come to terms with was that "he" was unfaithful. He had a lustful spirit and that his seed was a part of me as an inheritance, as Adam had passed sin down to us. The first sin being disobedience and then blame. And the man said, "the woman whom thou gavest to be with me, she gave me of the tree and I did eat. Genesis 3:12

Our disobedience is what God said not to do in His word. If a man also lie with mankind as he lieth with a woman, both of them have committed an abomination, they shall surely be put to death, their blood shall be upon them. Lev 20:13. Death represents the soul. It is separation from God. Behold all souls are mine; as the soul of the father, so also the soul of the son is mine; the soul that sinneth it shall die. Ezek 18:4

Chapter VII

One morning I heard a loud thump! I ran to the other room and there he was on the floor. The following week we received a phone call that a young man had died. The expression on his face was one of fear. Immediately my mind retraced an incident six months earlier when I was trying to contact him at his sister's house. This is where he indicated he was at the time. But each time I called, he wasn't there. He was sleeping with this young man and his sister was covering for him.

The young man was extremely attractive, and He had died from AIDS. My lover was experiencing chronic fatigue, high fevers and becoming sickly. Being in the health care field and working in the hospital with AIDS patients I knew what symptoms to look for. I asked him to let me look into his mouth. When he did this, I noticed his tongue was covered with fungus. I advised him to seek immediate medical attention. He was diagnosed with AIDS. Two weeks later he was dead. I stood alone with him in the room when he died. Thirteen years of friendship . . . . what now? Loneliness and Lost! As I walked from the hospital, the reality of my situation hit me. My security blanket had been taken away from me.

I would like to say that I cried out to God . . . . but I did not feel that God would hear me. I was still attending church, but I was in such deep pain. I dare not express the love I had for this man to the church. I couldn't tell anyone how much pain I was in, how empty my life was at this point, because no one would receive this abomination before the Lord. I was left in total darkness without a flashlight. Didn't know that all I needed to do was call on The Name of Jesus because there is power in that Name. Thought I was so deep in sin that He would not hear me. That He didn't want to hear me. Forgot that when you call on the Name of Jesus your circumstances change, that demons tremble, that nothing can separate you from His love . . . . so I walked away from His presence . . . .

I uprooted myself and moved to a new apartment and change began to take place. Still depressed, still grieving, I had lost the only person who I knew and loved for thirteen years. Not only did I lose him but I lost his family (whom I considered my family) as well. After his death, they never contacted me again. I sat alone for weeks in a very depressed emotional state of mind and no one called. I hadn't touched a drink or smoked any weed for over a year. I felt the need to have one drink, to ease the pain . . . just one drink.

As a dog returning to its vomit, so a fool returns to his folly. Pro 26:11. I began to medicate myself again with drugs and alcohol. I felt as if the church had forsaken me . . . the only family I knew had turned their backs on me and sometimes I felt as if God had forsaken me as well. He left me a substantial amount as his beneficiary. In church I began to sit further and further to the back on my way out. I was attending church intoxicated, smelling of alcohol. I had lost my joy in the Lord and finally I disappeared completely from the Body of Christ into my sinful lifestyle again. One night I was so intoxicated I fell asleep on my dining room floor listening to music. When I awoke, I still had the alcohol bottle between my legs the next morning. This is how I started my breakfast. I was waiting for someone to try to find me . . . guess what??? No one was looking for me . . . .

"When the unclean spirit is gone out of a man, he walketh through dry places seeking rest and fineth none. Then he saith, I will return into my house from whence I came out and when he is come, he findeth it empty, swept and garnished. Then goeth he and taketh with him seven other spirits more wicked then himself and they enter

in and dwell there; and the last state of that man is worse than the first. Even so shall it be also unto this wicked generation." Matthew 12: 43-45.

I had no remorse. My sexual addiction was in full force. The seven spirits that ambushed me were

- **LUST**
- **PRIDE**
- **DECEITFULNESS**
- **REBELLION,**
- **DRUNKEDNESS,**
- **HOMOSEXUALITY AND**
- **UNFORGIVENESS**.

Finally I was afforded a moment of sanity and decided to visit my doctor's office to determine if I was infected with the virus as well. This was a year after he had passed. I was positive. Later I spoke with a young man that I was seeing and explained to him that I was positive with the virus. His response was **"are we going to have sex or not?"** Why is light given to those in misery, and life to the bitter of soul, to those who long for death that does not come, who search for it more than for hidden treasure, who are filled with gladness and rejoice when they reach the grave? Why is life given to a man whose way is hidden, whom God has hedged in? Job 3:20-26 what I feared had come upon me; what I dreaded had happened to me. I have no peace, no quietness; I have no rest, but only turmoil.

In the back of my mind I was thinking who cares? His concern was not about the pain I was feeling, but whether we would indulge in sex or not. I thought obviously he is already positive and really did not care about either of us. We were both living in darkness and insanity using our sexual appetites to override our emotional need to be loved. The drugs would stimulate our bodies but our minds were filled with emptiness. As if the flesh have a mind of it's own. **The foolishness of men perverteth his ways and his heart fretteth against the Lord.** Prov 19:3.

Chapter VIII

When pride cometh, then cometh shame, but with the lowly is wisdom. The integrity of the upright shall guide them; but the perseverance of transgressors shall destroy them. Proverbs 11:2-3

One evening I set about cruising for drugs and sex. Satan had sent this young man my way at the right time. Whenever I committed a sexual act, I would have to be totally inebriated. The knowledge of God is a powerful force. I knew the act was distasteful to God, scorned by God, abhorred by God. I had to be high because I didn't want to know that God could see me when I made a mockery of His Name. I picked this brother up. He indicated that he had something I would like . . . something that would make what we were about to do feel even better. When he pulled it out, I knew what it was. I had convinced myself that

I would never try this drug. But I did. I obviously did not convince the enemy that I would never use it.

It was crack cocaine. When I pulled on that pipe (and because I was already an addict) it took me to another place. It took me to an illusionary hell. Satan showed me how good he could make me feel. I chased that first high for years. Suddenly while taking a shower, I had a strange taste in my mouth, a craving, a need and a desire for the drug. The search was on. I went looking for the guy who introduced me to this crack and as fate would have it . . . I found him. Of course I had to supply his high in exchange for his getting the drug for me. I was ashamed that I was in this place. A few months of crack and I had a prostitute, a drug dealer, which was for my need, and a relationship with a white boy with a drug habit stronger than mine living in my apartment. I received an eviction notice. I was going to work high and staying up all night long.

I couldn't stay awake or function on my job so my co-workers would cover for me. I was out of control. I decided to resign from my job. I lost my apartment and sold everything. I had $800.00 for my future. I sat with my sex partner and smoked up $500.00 of that $800.00. I sat in the middle of my living room floor and looked around at the empty apartment and my empty life. Consumed by so much pain and the repercussion of my sinful life.

The following day I packed all my remaining belongings in two large bags. My intent was to relocate to Maryland and begin anew. My friend and I decided to seek out more drugs. The $300.00 that I had left was burning a hole in my pockets. We stayed in a hotel room overnight, and while I was sleeping, he stole all of the money and left. I contacted his mother and she sent him back. He made arrangements for me to stay with his mother for a few days . . . ? Now herein lies the vision . . . . this was a white boy asking his mother if a black homosexual male could stay in her home for a few days? Imagine that . . . . and believe me, it was just a few days. At a private luncheon, his mother told him that she had purchased a ticket for me to Baltimore. She handed me a few extra bucks, dropped me off at the train station and said goodbye.

In Baltimore things changed temporarily. I stayed with my friend and her husband, got a job and did very well for myself. God was still faithful. I was still trying to find that personal, one on one relationship with God. I was back in church. Thinking that because I was in a different place (people, places and things) that life would be great. Unfortunately, in a minute, I learned that the drugs, and the pain, had all set up shop and was all waiting for me in Baltimore. It escalated when I found that my friend and her husband were crack heads! I started shouting again over my unholy stuff. After returning home one night from a party, totally smashed, I threw a pizza in the oven, still in the cardboard box and laid across the bed for what I thought was a minute, waiting for the pizza to heat up.

Suddenly there was very loud repeated knocking on my door. All the alarms in the building were going off. The Fire department came through the door and they were very angry. One of them open the oven and took the pizza out, open the porch door and tossed it. I was so embarrassed. The whole building had to be evacuated.

History repeats itself! I was on this roller coaster again, drinking and smoking excessively. It didn't matter where I indulged, at the bus stop or on the streets. I lied and feigned illness to my employer. The entire weekend would be spent with strangers, freaky sex acts and smoking drugs. At home the fridge was empty. I sat there, broke (because I had spent my entire check on drugs) hungry, sober and ashamed. Too ashamed to ask anyone for help. After the high, depression and reality always set in. "But your iniquities have separated between you and your God, and your sins have hid his face from you, that he will not hear." Isaiah 59:2.

On Monday I had to walk about six miles to work . . . in shame. I knew that my co-workers could see me walking. I made it to work on time. Later I spoke with the Director of Nursing and disclosed my drug addiction and that I was checking myself into rehab. With the assistance of my friend, I did just that. **Deal bountifully with thy servant, that I may live and keep thy Word**. Psalms 119:17.

After six weeks in rehab everything was going great. Of this one thing I was confident. Until I totally submitted my life to Christ there would be no permanent change. It is not until I came unto true repentance to God that transformation would begin. I would still be walking amongst the dead.

Again, I lost my apartment and was residing with friends. I was involved in the 12 step program with AA and NA. But I didn't take the first step towards Christ. After a few weeks I had a need, that same old desire showed itself. I found myself not going to meetings. Not only did I need healing from my drug addiction, but I needed deliverance from my lustful, sexual behavior. The meetings became meat markets or a possible place to meet someone. Sin did not come looking for me; I went in search of sin. I visited a bathhouse seeking fulfillment. I found something else altogether.

An older gentleman about sixty years old asked if he could step into my room, and I invited him in. Nothing happened because I was asking myself "what in the world would I do with this old man?"? I was 35 years old. We talked for a while and he asked if I would have breakfast with him? At first I declined and he left. Then I remembered that I didn't have money to get home and the spirit of manipulation came into play. I dressed quickly and I caught him before he left the bathhouse. When we arrived at the train station and stood in line, I acted as if I could not find my train ticket. (I never had one). I knew he would buy my ticket. After breakfast, we went by the place he was staying which was the Hyatt Regency. My first thought was how did this man have the money to stay in such an expensive hotel? He had no idea what was about to come.

Glass elevators and plush surroundings. In his room, sitting over in the corner was a mini bar. The thief cometh not but for to steal, kill and to destroy. John 10:10. Would you like a drink? I told him that I did not drink because I was a recovering addict. I was trying to save the man from what was to come if I took even a small drink . . . The enemy looked at me and said that it was all in my mind. What he was doing was manipulative. He wanted to get me drunk so that I would have sex with him and believe me, I would need to be comatose to engage in sex with him. I took a drink from the bar and it opened the door for more demons.

After work every day I would stop by his place to have a drink. One day he wasn't home and he left me money to go out to dinner. I had a few drinks and went out to dinner drunk. I found myself living more at his place than my own. I was not in love with this man and he knew this. But his plan was to have a young man as his sex toy and he knew it would be costly. But I had a plan. I thought like any other young man. I had a commodity that was in demand. I would use this to support me and my habit. I needed a sugar daddy that was willing to take care of me. My thoughts were why give it up for free when someone was willing to pay for it. There is a name that the world had for this type of exchange . . . . oh yes . . . . prostitution.

Even in our sinful behavior there were boundaries that you did not cross, things that we will and will not do. The thing that I did not like about him was that he was an unbeliever and an ungodly man. But my selfish, wicked and vain personality proved too much for him. The one thing that I knew that he did not know was that there was a GOD, and even in my wickedness I feared HIM. Five more spirits had attached itself to my already seven spirits. PROSTITUTION, SELFISHNESS, VANITY, MANIPULATION and GREED. Savior . . . . please doesn't pass me by . . . .

Chapter IX

I went to visit and tried to get into his place but there was no answer. Weird . . . . the key did not work in the door. When he arrived, he told me that he had been evicted from the hotel. He needed a place to stay. He moved in with a friend and me and promised that we would not be staying there long because we would be moving to his home in Chicago. He flew to Chicago for a visit to take care of family business. He had no idea I was smoking crack. Things were changing. I was looking like a kept man. He indicated that by the following week we would be moving. It was an apartment building. I was so excited. We packed our belongings and shipped them to Chicago ahead of us. **The spirit of a man will sustain his infirmity; but a wounded spirit who can bear?** Proverbs 18:14.

He decided to leave a few days ahead of me because he had to meet with his daughters and attend a funeral. It was Ramsey Lewis' mother funeral. When I arrived a friend drove us to downtown Chicago. As we drove around I noticed how beautiful and clean this Chi-Town was. We walked, literally walked, from downtown to the Southside of Chicago. Strange . . . . why are we not taking a cab or at best, the subway? I asked myself . . . . what have I gotten myself into? I was exhausted! O my God, I was in for the surprise of my life!!! When we arrived at the building, he had no keys and the building looked abandoned. He asked me to climb through the window to let him in. I was praying this was his building. It was only by the grace of God that I wasn't arrested for Trespassing or Breaking and Entering. I was not aware that he was living on his wife's insurance and her social security benefits.

The building was in arbitration with the courts. It was obvious he had his own pain. He had lost his wife to cancer and had two college age daughters. He didn't want to have another heterosexual relationship because it meant he was being unfaithful to his wife. He had lost all faith in God. He was a very sad man.

My drug and sexual addiction was escalating and I began visiting bathhouses and indulging in promiscuity. I needed to feel wanted and I felt in control through my sexual perversion. While he slept at night, I would steal his money for crack. I became a thief and a great liar. All of this resulting from a father's rejection and the uncertainty of who I was created to be. My body was being used as a sexual tool to please other men who were also rejected, abused, raped and forgotten by society and the church community. Weeks passed and a bang at the door startled me. There stood the sheriff waiting to evict us. They asked if there were any guns in the house? I said no. I had just awakened and I was so confused.

They came in and immediately started moving our belongings out of the house and sitting them on the streets. When he returned home, he found his belongings on the streets. I could see the pain in his eyes. My thoughts . . . what now? I had started going back to church at the Apostolic Church of God under a great Pastor, Bishop Arthur Brazier. He had reached out to help me. I had also joined the Coral Men's choir. He asked a friend if I could stay with her for the night and she agreed for just that one night. That Sunday, I invited her and her family to church. They accepted Jesus Christ as Lord and Savior on that day. He returned for me the next day and we took the train to the North side. We were homeless. We walked the street until midnight and signed ourselves into a bathhouse.

The next day we found a transit hotel, (Diplomat) but there were no rooms available. The young man told us to come back the next day and he would have a room for us. We walked around until we found a dirty, roached infested motel for the night. I had to put plastic slippers on to protect my feet in the shower. This was a long way from the Hyatt. Even though I was going through this, I knew that God had not forgotten about me because I certainly had not forgotten about HIM. I was living a life of Hell. I was like David. I knew that God would not leave my soul in hell. **For thou will not leave my soul in hell, neither will thou suffer thine Holy One to see corruption.** Psalm 16:10.

I continued to attend church and to seek His face, until I went into the prayer room at Apostolic and a young lady called me to the side and asked "did I know that this was a special prayer room?" In essence, not anyone could be in the prayer room. Obviously it was an anointed prayer room and only the righteous of the righteous could enter in. I was totally taken aback! I was in shock, and excused myself. If she could see in the Spirit that I was calling on the Lord . . . . I was fighting for my life and for my soul!! This is no reflection of Bishop Brazier because I know he had no idea that this was happening in his church! This sister was powerless, clueless and in need to assert authority in some arena. The prayer room was not that place. How many souls had she run away from God and from the church? I never returned to Apostolic again. The Spirit of Rejection has always followed me. With the drugs, I could numb the pain and when I had sex with men, I could make pretend that I am with someone who just loves me for me . . . if just for those few moments. I was in the arms of someone that loved and cared about me . . . . even though it was an illusion. I was still in my mess, but I was still seeking God.

We returned to the Diplomat hotel and obtained the room as previously promised. As always I was able to find a high. After we had been there for a minute, I told him I needed a place where I would be able to cook. I was receiving my social security disability check by this time and we heard of a hotel in the neighborhood with studios apartments. I took a trip back to NY for a small vacation. I went searching for an old fling, but couldn't find him. I drank, smoked and partied at clubs. It didn't even occur to me that all of my friends had died or were dying of AIDS.

Returning home he asked about my well-being? I told him I was all right. He said" I want you to get checked out because they said I have the HIV virus. I confessed to him that I was in denial of being HIV positive. When I told him that I had lost my lover to the disease, I thought that he would question me but he did not. I found that disturbing. Were we both on a mission to self destruct? He, because of his wife and I because of my lover? We visited bathhouses and had unprotected sex with other men. He missed his wife so much that he didn't care about being HIV positive. I finally returned to the doctor and took a blood test.

My results came back with a viral load in the thousands and a CD4 count of 200. I had an AIDS diagnosis. I understood what the scripture meant when it said, 'the wages of sin is death; but the gift of God is eternal life through Jesus Christ our Lord. Romans 6:23.

I realized that I was separated from God . . . this was my spiritual death. The AIDS diagnosis indicated my physical death was very near. How many had I infected? How many had re-infected me with different strains of the virus? Depression set in. When I returned from the doctor's appointment, he indicated he was going on vacation. I thought great!! He said "I am leaving you $100.00 and my cash card. If you need anything go into the bank and get it". A week passed and he called. He was staying another week. Another week passed and I called the number he had given me but no answer. I became concerned about him, but more about myself. I had spent all of my money. I decided to go to the bank and withdraw some cash. I inserted the card and the card was sucked in and never returned.

I had spent all of my money on drugs and now I could not withdraw any money from his account. I felt betrayed and abandoned. I had relocated all the way out here to Chicago, didn't know anybody, had no friends, no money, a drug habit and AIDS. I walked the streets looking for drugs and there was always someone smoking. I didn't have money for a pack of cigarettes. It was God's great love and mercy that allowed me to live. Of that one thing I am very sure. He never returned and I never heard from him again to this day. I didn't know it, but God's plan for me was in motion.

I would often think about what my eternity would look like. It didn't look that great. The question for me was, had I chosen the eternity that Christ have prepared for me, the eternity that He had promised me in His Word, or did I choose the eternity like the rich man chose that ended up in hell? The rich man went to hell and in hell he lifted up his eyes being in torment? Luke 16:23. How long had he been in hell? I thought about judgment day, when God will call them up from hell to stand before His presence to judge them in that place. Imagine standing before God, in His presence, peace and the fullness of His Love, and an overwhelming joy comes over you, and then you find yourself standing before His wrath begging for mercy and being judged. You are returned to your torment for eternity.

And the sea gave up the dead which were in it; and death and hell delivered up the dead which were in them: and they were judged every man according to their works. This is the second death. Rev 20:13

Chapter X

Within a month I was visiting the Catholic Charities food pantry, standing in line with other homeless people. I would return to the hotel with bagged groceries with no idea what was in them. But trust me, I was grateful. Reality set in that he was not coming back. I had no one to put my trust in but God. The hotel was in Boys Town, a gay community, the gay belt of the Midwest. Drugs were readily available. I was thinking that I really needed to change my life and I knew this could only happen through God. How did I get to this place? Satan was really fighting hard against me, my soul was restless and it seemed like I was running out of time. O wretched man that I am! Who shall deliver me from the body of this death? Romans 7:24. I could not run from it. It was there! Temptation was everywhere.

I received my disability check and I convinced myself that I was not going to spend my check on drugs. I was going to pay my rent, food and medication. There I was in the kitchen preparing green peppers and onions, when my addiction summoned me. I fought as hard as I could. Out the door and on a three day high. When I returned home, I was broke. The rent, food and medications were on hold again. Green peppers with the onion and the knife were exactly where I had left them. I lay across my bed and I could feel my heart racing. I just wanted to give up . . . go to sleep and die, but I knew that my soul would spend eternity in Hell. The sorrow of Hell encompassed me about. The snares of Death prevented me. Psalms 18:5. I was so fearful. I pulled myself together and decided to seek help. I knew of a rehab center that accepted walk-ins, if room were available. When I arrived, they immediately checked my vital signs. I was referred to the emergency room. My blood pressure was 210/110 and my heart rate was 130 per minute. The transportation provided was a van that was dropping off young men at various locations. I was calling on Jesus the whole time to please spare my life. I had no one but God.

Finally we arrived at Cook County hospital. I gave the nurse my name and it seemed like I was waiting forever. I advised the nurse of my chest pain. Her reaction was unexpected. Her facial expression was one of disgust as she instructed me to sit down and wait for my name to be called. Earlier when she asked what brought me in, I told her I had smoked too much crack. I assume she had no great love for a crack head. Following my release from an overnight stay in the hospital, a young man sitting next to me on the train was trying to convince me to allow him to go home with me. I said no. Herein is a glimpse into my insanity. As soon as I returned home the young lady down the hall offered me some crack. I smoked it and there I was running with her to find more. We spent all night looking for more. But Glory be to God when I returned to Rehab the next day I was finally ready to redeem my ticket to come home to my Father's kingdom. I was like the Prodigal Son when he thought to himself, I will arise and go to my father, and will say unto him, Father, I have sinned against heaven, and before thee. Luke 15:18

Change had finally come. Two weeks in rehab had afforded me time to sit at my Savior's feet. When I returned home, I didn't waste any time gathering information on outpatient drug care centers. I had to report to counseling every Monday, Wednesday and Friday. I was very excited about new beginnings. There was a church a block away called Faith Tabernacle Church. Just a few weeks before he left, I told him that I was going to visit that church one day. He said very sarcastically, "Well, why don't you?" I had yet to visit that church. I didn't know Jesus was patiently waiting for me there. He keeps His promises and He is faithful.

All that I had ask of Him and that He promised me in His Word, was waiting for me to arrive. My deliverance was waiting for me. My healing couldn't wait for me to get there, Freedom was speaking my name. The spirit kept urging me to come.

How bad did I want it? Monday evening I walked to the Outpatient Clinic which was about a mile to walk. I didn't have any money, but His Grace was sufficient enough for me. I walked to that clinic, to and fro for two weeks. On the weekends I would sit outside my window on the fire escape and watch everyone enjoying themselves. I knew that if I walked into a bar, my nightmare would repeat itself. I needed God and God only to help me deal with my pain. I needed Him to show me the seed that was deposited in my spirit and how it took root. Who watered and nourished the root until it grew and flourished into this homosexual behavior? I was using drugs so that I could suppress the pain of self hatred. My first great visitation from God was audible. I heard his voice tell me when I went to the clinic that night; tell the counselor that He had healed me. I thought to myself that this was the enemy speaking to me, but somehow deep down inside of my knower I was assured that this was God. Faith without works is dead.

When I arrived, I did just as the Lord had instructed me. I could feel the Holy Spirit pushing me. I said, "Excuse me. The Lord told me that He has healed me. The counselor responded, as if I were a psych patient, "that's nice Roger, but I think that you need to keep coming". I said "no thank you and you have a good night" and walked out. Sixteen years later, to this day, I have not returned and I have maintained my sobriety, alcohol and drug free. God admires those whose faith has been tested and remains true. 1 Peter 1:7 These trials are only to test your faith, to show that it is strong and pure. It is being tested as fire tests and purifies gold—and your faith is far more precious to God than mere gold. If your faith remains strong after being tested by fiery trials, it will bring you much praise and glory and honor on the day when Jesus Christ is revealed to the whole world.

From this experience I learned that Faith pleases God. It was by His Grace and my faith in Christ Jesus that allowed me to have a free, joyful and spiritual life from drugs and from homosexual behavior. When I hear others ask the question "will God love us?" The question is not whether God loves us. He has proven His love from Alpha. The question is do we love God? Do we love Him enough to give our very best and allow His Will to be done in our lives? To avoid sin, to the best of our abilities and live saved, sanctified and sin free. What we are really saying is that God loves us so much that we can live a sinful life irregardless that He sent His Son Jesus to earth to be beaten and to die for us. We think God will wink at our sin. We are saying that we can continue to commit adultery, fortification, homosexuality and lie. So what? Even though He has said and proven that He Whom the Son sets free, is free indeed and that man should not live by bread alone but by every word that proceedeth out of the mouth of God. Do you really love God? Are you really a believer? Do you really believe His Word from Genesis to Revelations or are you merely going through the motions of church goers? Are you really free or are you just free on Sundays? The rest of the week you are bound by your addictions, your habits and your behaviors? Are your Pastors keeping you bound so that you will need them as opposed to needing God? Looking towards leadership and not looking towards the Lord? Search your heart and be sure it is God centered and not self centered.

In 1997 I kept the promise to myself to visit that church a block away. I met the Lord there. He was still waiting. I went to Howard Browns thrift store and purchased a jacket and a pair of pants for church. On Sunday morning, I went to Faith Tabernacle Church. I enjoyed the service even though I was still struggling with homosexuality. During service I begin to feel the presence of God in my life again. In the gay community I tried to convince myself that it was okay to attend a gay church service. I never felt the presence of the Lord. I even went to see a gay therapist to help me understand my life. He never questioned any sexuality I experienced as a child. I believe this is an area that the gay lifestyle avoid in fear of finding some child abuse issues. You will find yourself marinating in the lust of the lifestyle, which brings about the spirit of idolatry. It was at this time when I realized that I worshipped the lifestyle more than I worshipped God. I had a spirit of rebellion and I was being disobedient to the Word of God. I believe this is why all of my friends have perished. Anything done in disobedience must die.

Thou shall not lie with mankind as womankind. It is an abomination (Leviticus 18:22) If a man also lie with mankind as he lieth with a woman, both of them have committed an abomination; they shall surely be put to death; their blood shall be upon them (Lev 20:13). People always say that this is the old testament, but God said, JESUS CHRIST IS THE SAME, YESTERDAY, TODAY AND FOREVERMORE!!! (Heb 13:8) So shall my Word that goeth forth out of my mouth; it shall not return unto me void, but it shall accomplish that which I please and I shall prosper in the thing where I sent it. (Isa 55:11) After receiving knowledge of the Word of God, I realized that I was powerless over my homosexuality. God is true and I was a liar. I was a sinner that needed to be saved by the gift of Grace that God so freely gives.

Chapter XI

While attending an outside camp meeting at church, the enemy tried to convince me that I was lost and that I had been here before. I had tried this church thing repeatedly and it seemingly, did not work for me. So the prince of the pits, tried to deceive me and convince me that there was no hope. There is always hope in Jesus Christ. As long as there is hope, I could find my way back to Jesus. Still confused and struggling with my life, I continued worshipping and praising God. Sunday morning, I sat in the back of the church. Bishop Ray Llarena spoke these words that began the transformation in my life. He said that "God loves the sinner but He hates the sin." I had heard these words before, but never received revelation of the significance of these words. *God loves the sinner, which means that God loves me, with all my flaws and all of my mess . . . but He hates the sin . . . He hates the act of homosexuality;*

he hates the perverted choices that I made. God
loves me, but He hates my sinful ways. But the power
behind the message was that "God loves me"!!! The
sinner man needs to know this. God loves you in all
of your sewage. God loves you in all of your mess.
God loves you in your drunkenness, your filth, your
addictions, vomit, your brokenness, God loves you.
His Son did not die exclusively for those working the
altar in the church; He was bruised for you too. The
altar was opened and people went down to the altar to
repent, to leave whatever at the altar . . . except me.
I stood where I was, where I received His revelation
and I spoke to God from my heart. I told the Lord, "I
have been down to that altar too many times. Hands
have been laid on me, I have fallen in the spirit and
I have been baptized three times. If change is going
to come, it will have to come from this place. I will
not go down to the altar again, instead, I will come
to you as a child and ask your forgiveness. I repent.
Will you please show me your mercy and grace over
my life"? In that instance I felt the change within my
heart. In true repentance is instant change. When I
left the church, my heart was changed, but my walk,
my character were still the same. But God was starting
a work in me from the inside.

Being confident of this very thing, that He which
hath begun a good work in you will perform it until
the day of Jesus Christ. (Phil 1:6). My soul rejoice to
know that the Holy Spirit will keep me until the day of

our Lord and Savior return then we can recite Psalm 107:2 Let the redeemed of the Lord say so, whom he hath redeemed from the hands of the enemy. Praise God I AM REDEEMED!!!!

While reading my bible the voice of the Lord came to me and said "open up Isa 45", and my eyes fell to verse 1-3 . . . I keep His word with me until this day. "Thus saith the Lord to His anointed, to Cyrus whose right hand I have holden; to subdue nations before him; and I will loose the loins of kings to open before him the two leaven gates; and the gates shall not be shut. I will go before thee and make the crooked places straight. I will break in pieces the gates of brass and cut in sunder the bars of iron. And I will give thee the treasures of darkness and hidden riches of secret places that thou mayest know that I, the Lord which call thee by thy name **Roger** (I made that thing personal) I am the God of Israel.

And God is faithful in His promises. **The Brass** represented the **idolatry** I was committing in my life. The open **Iron Gate** that will never be shut again is the gates that released me from the enemies hand and the prison that he had me in. The **Crooked Path** was my mind in a confused state of who God created me to be and he straightened it out that I should walk in the path of righteousness, and the hidden darkness of his treasures is **His Word** in my heart to replace the ungodly, deceitful and evilness that brought me to salvation. Today, I do know that He is the God of Israel and He calls me by my name.

The following week I was thrust into spiritual warfare. There was a young man who lived in the same hotel as myself. I had a lustful spirit for him. He indicated he had heard that I was going back to church and could I come to his room and talk to him. Look at the enemy!!!! I picked up my bible (I just knew I was doing the Will of God), followed him to his room and he begin to tell me that he was fighting his drug addiction. As I begin to minister and tell him what God had did for me, he pulled out his pipe and lite it in front of me. I picked up my bible and ran for my life! I asked God to please help me and I heard God as plain as day ask . . . . Who sent you? Who sent you to that room? Did you seek my face before you took off toting your bible? From thenceforth I stayed in my room, went to church and faithfully went to bible study on Wednesday nights and Foundation of Faith on Saturdays. I was in church so much I went to kiddie bible study. I was not going to allow the enemy to catch me off guard like that again.

I completed the six weeks requirement of the Foundation of Faith classes. There were several very steadfast and solid sisters in the class and Pastor Kenneth Barnett, who later performed my wedding. He asked if anyone had comments about the class and to testify to the glory of what God had did for them.

When I opened up my mouth, the words that spilled forth were pushed out by the Holy Spirit. I had no intentions of making this confession. 'God has delivered me from the lifestyle of homosexuality"! The shame of the confession was overpowering. I was awaiting a negative response. Everyone grabbed me and hugged me. That's when I realized that God had a purpose for my life. Someone informed the Bishop about my testimony. That Sunday morning during service, the Bishop announced that a young man was delivered from homosexuality and he spoke into my life. He was the first man to deposit a positive message into my spirit. He said these words that set my new life with Christ in motion. "God has great things for you". At that moment I knew that I had become an overcomer. And they overcame him (satan) by the blood of Jesus and the word of their testimony: and they loved not their lives unto the death. (Revelations 12:11).

I learned that my life was not my own anymore. Walking in humility is my garment and my shame is in my past. But walking in victory gives my Big God honor. For I am not ashamed of the gospel of Jesus Christ; for it is the power of God unto salvation to everyone that believeth; to the Jew first and also to the Greek. For therein is the righteousness of God revealed from faith to faith as it is written, the just shall live by faith. Romans 1:16-17. I am the just and I live by faith and faith alone.

After thirty-two years of homosexuality, I realized that I needed to make many changes in my life. II Cor 5:17 states, therefore if any man be in Christ Jesus, he is a new creature. Old things are passed away, behold, all things are become new. At that moment I did not feel as if I was a new creature. I had the same vices. There were people in the church and they had their doubts. The saints still made negative comments after I confessed my deliverance. They commented about my walk and questioned my deliverance. Don't count on the saints to believe God for you. You'd better believe and know God for yourself! They have no idea of what deliverance looks like . . . . and neither did I. I had no idea what it meant to be a man. Would the desire for same sex relationships ever go away? How will I deal with my old gay friends? Did I want a male/female relationship? Did I want to get married? How would that woman want and deal with a man that had been in the homosexual lifestyle? Will she throw that in my face when she gets angry? Am I man enough for her? How will people expect me to act in the church knowing that I am HIV positive? Can I really live a straight life? It is difficult to change our nature, because our nature is sinful. Among whom also we all had our conversation in times past in the lust of our flesh, fulfilling the desires of the flesh and of the mind; and were by nature the children of wrath, even as others. (Eph 2:3).

I began to think about how difficult it would be to leave my past life behind me, the life we know, the life we are comfortable with. Our friends, family and ungodly habits. In Genesis 19, the angel of the Lord told Lot's family not to look back. You know the story. She looked back because she had unfinished business there, her friends, her home, family and memories. She didn't trust God in what He had prepared for her and her family. She left two motherless daughters and the enemy crept in and caused them to commit incest with their father through the spirit of drunkenness. But God himself worked it out for my own good. Romans 8:28 And we know that all things work together for the good of them that love God, to them who are the called according to his purpose

Today when I think about the price that Jesus Christ paid for me, I am confident that it was not the nails or the suffering that kept Him on the cross. But His unfailing love and forgiveness He had for us. He opened the gate to eternal life that we may go from death to life. For a moment he felt forsaken but, He completed the task, hung His head and died . . . . for me. He did this for us. But He that shall endure unto the end the same shall be saved. Matt 24:14. Blessed is the Name of the Lord. Now I understood that I needed a renewed mind and complete submission to Christ. To put Gods' sword down on the inside of me and begin a personal relationship with him. Isa 55:7-8 Let the wicked forsake his way and the unrighteous man his thoughts, and let him return unto the Lord, and He will have mercy upon him; and to our God, for He will abundantly pardon. For my thoughts are not your thoughts; neither are your ways my ways saith the Lord. He suffered that we might be able to commune with God and return to right fellowship with Him. He was wounded for our transgressions and bruised for our iniquities, the chastisement of our peace was upon him and with his stripes we are healed. Isa 53:5.

Chapter XII

The question is why should He not send me to hell when He has given me the blueprint to live right? I only need to have faith in His Son. Many times my soul cried out for Him, but I felt as if He had taken His Holy Spirit away from me. Thank God for grace and mercy. I can openly confess that had it not been for the Lord who is on my side, my sins would have consumed me.

I wanted the kind of relationship with God that others had with Him. Most people who experienced drug addiction, alcoholism, and homosexuality, didn't want to remember the pain those behaviors caused them. The molestation, the rapes, not just the physical pain, but the emotional and mental turmoil. The negativity that was fed into your spirit, "you are to dark, to fat, to yellow". You will never be worth anything when you grow up! All negative seeds. You begin to seek out people and places where you are accepted. You become comfortable in that situation and can find excuses for why you are the way you are. When TRUTH comes and tells you who and what you are, that is the moment when change begins. Some choose to stay in their comfort zone because of the pain.

We think that we are changing for people, but we are really changing to please God. There are two important things to take from God's Word about oneself. (Ephesians 1:4) According as He hath chosen us in Him before the foundation of the world, that we should be holy and without blame before Him in love. Through all my mess Jesus died on the Cross for me because He knew who and what I would become. I am called for a purpose. The world was not even formed yet, but I was on His mind, all I had to do accept Christ and He promised to do the rest.

Secondly, 1Corithians 1:27 But God has chosen the foolish things of the world to confound the wise, and God hath chosen the weak things of the world to confound the things which are mighty. Moses was a murderer, David was a murderer and adultery, Abraham was a liar, Rahab was a prostitute, but God used these empty vessels. My drug addiction and sexual behavior was foolish. God's Word has made me wise through His Truth. I had problems giving God control of my life. Because of the issues in my life it proved difficult to allow God to have complete control. When we decide to give our lives to Christ, we think that we have to give up so much. The reality is that you don't have to give up anything. When you experience the love of God, you will want to give up your unholy stuff. God will replace that unholy stuff with joy; the unspeakable joy . . . . that's deep within your soul . . . . the peace in knowing that it is well with your soul.

God is to me what and how He has exposed Himself to me. (John 1:14) And the Word was made flesh and dwelt amongst us and we beheld His Glory, the Glory of the only begotten of the Father, full of Grace and Truth. It is the grace of God that allows me to live today and His Truth that is keeping me.

I had to accept that I was a sinner before I could be healed. God knows what you are. You need to know and confess who and what you are. Whenever our Lord speaks about sin, he is very precise. When He speaks about healing He is very clear. Once healing began I realized that I served a God with purpose. He created everything with purpose . . . especially man. When God created man, He created man in His own image. ***There was nothing after His Kind.*** Male and female made He them. And God blessed them and God said unto them "Be fruitful and multiply" An apple tree brings forth apples, a fish bring forth fish and a human being brings forth another human being. The seed that God planted in His creation has purpose.

Romans 1:20 states, for the invisible things of Him (God) from the creation of the world are clearly seen (purpose) being understood by the things that are made (purpose) even His eternal power and "Godhead" so that they are without excuse, because God purpose and plan was so perfect from the very beginning we have no excuse.

We know that the seed that God has planted in man and woman is to pro-create . . . to multiply. What seed does Homosexuality pro-create and multiply?

- Un-thankfulness
- Vanity
- Foolishness
- To be wise and became fools
- Uncleanliness
- Lustfulness
- Dishonor their bodies
- Liars
- Idolatry (serve the creature more than the creator)
- Vile affection
- Change the nature of
- Burn in their lust
- No knowledge of God
- Reprobate mind
- Unrighteousness
- Fornication
- Wickedness

- Covetousness
- Maliciousness
- Envy
- Murder
- Debate
- Malignancy
- Whisperer
- Back biter
- Hater of God
- Deceitful
- Proud
- Boaster
- Inventor of Evil Things
- Without understanding
- Covenant breaker
- Without natural affection
- Implacable
- Unmerciful

His thoughts of homosexuality are sinful and His ways are Holy. If His mercy, grace, love and the Blood of His Son Jesus was removed from us what would God see? We would have to run and hide ourselves as Adam and Eve did when their eyes were opened. We would realize how naked we are in front of God. They knew that their eyes were opened to sin and they were children of disobedience. God said don't do it and we did it anyway. A man shall not lay with a man as with a woman and so when I did that, I was being disobedient which is transgression. Jeremiah 3:13 tells us to "Only acknowledge thine iniquity that thou has transgressed against the Lord thy God and hast scattered thy ways to the strangers under every green tree, and ye have not obeyed my voice saith the Lord."

The purpose that God had for my life was in place before the foundation of the world. His perfect will allowed me to go through this journey in my life for His Glory. His presence was there when my birth father (not my biological father) raped me. He wept for me, but it was part of the process. He was there when I made a decision to smoke crack cocaine. He was there when I found myself homeless in a strange city. He was there when I received my AIDS diagnosis, the same way He was there when His Son was crucified for us. I was sanctified for His great and divine purpose. He was there, and he sat back and allowed it to happen, and just when things seemed hopeless, He snatched me up out of it . . . . for His glory! Just when I thought all hope was gone, He said "see, this is why I allowed you to go through what you went through, because where I AM sending you to, you needed to go through this. I had to equip you for where and who I am sending you to. Before I formed thee in the belly, I knew thee and before thou camest forth out of the womb, I sanctified thee and ordained thee a prophet unto the nations. Jeremiah 1:5.

Show me in the bible where homosexuality is not a sin? I can show you that He loves the homosexual, fornicator, adulterer, liar because He died for our sins that we may be forgiven through repentance and a renewal of the mind. There were times that I used my sexuality to express my worthlessness as a man. The drugs helped me to become detached from my reality of what I was and allowed me to become emotionless. I totally understood that the life I was living was not in order with the word of God. What shall we say then? Shall we continue in sin, that grace may abound? God forbid, how shall we that are dead to sin, live any longer therein. Romans 6:1-2. Most people have experienced a passing thought about a homosexual encounter with a man or a woman. Why, because our thoughts are wicked and because sin in our nature. There are those that struggle with homosexuality even now because it is a stronghold, it is bondage and not easily conquered. Our thought pattern needs to change from being born to being BORN AGAIN. Do not fear . . . you are not alone . . . You are made in the image of a Perfect God. Do not underestimate the spirit of homosexuality. Most people think they know how to deliver the homosexual, but man cannot deliver the homosexual, only God can. Wisdom has to come from God.

Ephesians 6:12 For we wrestle not against flesh and blood, but against principalities, against powers, against the rulers of the darkness of this world, against spiritual wickedness in high places. Those who are in agreement with same sex marriage and those who participate in homosexuality, our congressmen, clergy, lawyers, judges, all those who say yes . . . GOD says no! People are so fascinated with the lifestyle of homosexuality, especially Christians. We are now told to celebrate and accept this lifestyle. Most would say they are bi-sexual and not gay. Gay is a term, homosexuality is a sexual act. An individual's preference does not afford the right to pressure a person to use their rectum for one's sexual need, or their mouths for pleasure. God created us to taste and eat with our tongues and mouth. Everything God made has a purpose.

Who knows the judgment of God that they commit such things and are worthy of death (separation from God's love in eternity). Not only do others do the same but those that commit such acts find pleasure in doing them. God's purpose and plan for our lives is much greater than this.

Chapter XIII

No weapon that is formed against thee shall prosper; and every tongue that shall rise against thee in judgment thou shalt condemn. This is the heritage of the servants of the Lord, and their righteousness is of me saith the Lord. Isaiah 54:17

We were invited to speak on an HIV/AIDS panel at a well established church in Chicago. The facilitator asked each person to give a brief introduction. There were four of us, two men and two women. I shared briefly about my HIV diagnosis and my deliverance from the homosexual lifestyle. My wife followed. Next a young man spoke, and stated he was an active homosexual. He did not agree with my beliefs regarding homosexuality, and he had a lover. You know the devil does not like the truth. After the panel discussion, he approached me clothed with the spirit of manipulation. He said it was ok to be gay that God loves us all. I smiled and told him I agreed with him, God does love us all. I did not want to debate with this young man. He leaned over and decided to rearrange my tie. He told my wife, "I gave your husband my phone number just in case you don't give it to him." My wife, being the Godly woman that she is smiled and stated, "that's fine". This was on a Friday. That Monday morning my wife received a phone call from the facilitator stating that one of the men that had participated on the panel had died over the weekend. Is your husband okay? My wife responded 'yes, I just dropped him off at his job". My wife called and informed me that the young man had run across the median on the interstate straight into a garbage truck, and died instantly. Touch not mine anointed and do my prophets no harm. Psalms 105:15

First, that young man should not have debated with me concerning my deliverance. I was giving God His Glory and Honor. Next, touching me was blatant disrespect not only to me, but to the true and living God, offering me his phone number for immoral purposes. And then he disrespected a sacred and holy marriage that God Himself ordained, a marriage which truly represents Christ and His Church. This young man dishonored God, His Word and what God stands for . . . Holiness.

In Romans it speaks about how homosexuality does two things that displeases God. Romans 1:30 states they are inventors of evil things and second, Romans 1:25 tells us they have themselves mutilated and attempt to substitute a penis and/or vagina to please the lust of their flesh. What I find hypocritical is that if one is happy about being gay, why would you want to change your sexual identity? Does one really want to be a heterosexual? You are already a heterosexual. You decided to continue in the act of sodomy. In striving to establish open communications with the LBGT community, I attended several communication workshops. The workshops were powerful and there were very teachable moments. One interesting phenomenon was the transgender breakout session. I learned that most transgendered individuals have transformed themselves from the neck to the waist, but remain either male or female from the waist down, awaiting a better product to be put on the market. One thing that God does not do is do anything half way. He is a God of wholeness. It proved amazing that the transgendered individual did not empathize with the confusion, pain and lost to his/her parents. They had lost a son or daughter and were in the grieving process. Selfishness indicates I expect you (the parents) to accept and receive me because it is a personal choice that I made. Anger (on the parent's behalf) indicates, I am grieving the loss of a child. Anger is one of the stages of grieving.

Anger—why can't the child accept who God created them to be, either male or female?

Denial—denying that the child has actually chosen to be gay and to transform themselves into other than what God made them.

Bargaining—God, if you would heal my child and make him/her be just like any normal child and forget about this gay thing, I will serve only you.

Depression—this cannot be, please don't allow me to lose my child to this lifestyle.

Acceptance—I haven't lost a son but I have gained a daughter.

How strong is the spirit of rejection and the need for acceptance? It causes a young man to desire to castrate himself voluntarily. He wants to inject female hormones into the Glory of God. She has a consented, unnecessary double mastectomy and disposes of her womb which God has given to carry life. She flushes out nations from her womb. Deut. 23:1 He that is wounded in the stones, or hath his privy member cut off, shall not enter into the congregation of the Lord.

For many years I denied that God was calling me into my purpose. Spiritually I was not in tune with God. He was calling my name out of the depths of the grave. Here I am. The signs were evident of my tormented life. The death of a man I loved, homelessness, drug addiction and an AIDS diagnosis. He spoke into my spirit, healing and deliverance is waiting for you. For whosoever calls on the Name of the Lord, shall be saved. But my soul was not prepared for warfare against the demons that stalked and tormented me. My need for acceptance, love and the deep rooted pain of my past remained. I refused to come out of my grave clothes. That would mean that I would not be able to accept forgiveness for myself. Life would emerge from within me. I would no longer be able to walk among the tombstones with the names of my friends and past that lead me there. **Romans 5:1-5** Therefore, since we have been justified through faith, we have peace with God through our Lord Jesus Christ, through whom we have gained access by faith into this grace in which we now stand. And we rejoice in the hope of the glory of God. Not only so, but we also rejoice in our sufferings, because we know that suffering produces perseverance; perseverance, character; and character, hope. And hope does not disappoint us, because God has poured out his love into our hearts by the Holy Spirit, whom he has given us. Who would not serve a God like that? O taste and see that the Lord, he is good! God has put it in my heart to reach out to all those who are lost, regardless of who you are. God has proven his love for you. My life is no longer mine own. It is Christ and Christ alone. I walk in the spirit of humility. The fear of the Lord is the instruction of wisdom; and before honor is humility. (Proverbs 15:33)

Today I am married to a wonderful wife. We are both Pastors. God has allowed us to form a ministry called the Ford Foundation/Outreach Ministry. We work with young men and women that are HIV positive and struggling with the lifestyle of homosexuality. He is a God that will restore, heal and set free. I am that foolish thing that God has chosen and within my weakness he made me strong by His Word. The mightiness of His Word has changed my life. Yes satan rears his ugly head and tests me, but His grace is sufficient enough for me. For God has left a thorn in my side to remind me, "before I was afflicted I went astray, but now have I kept thy word." Psalm 119:67. I remember His Word so that I won't forget that His will is what is best for me. I will never trust myself, because the flesh has a mind of its own. It will come against the will of God. Sin feels good. But God's righteousness is revealed from heaven. Know ye not that the unrighteous shall not inherit the kingdom of God?

Be not deceived: neither fornicators, nor idolators, nor adulters, nor effeminate, nor abusers of themselves with mankind, nor thieves, nor covetous, nor drunkards, nor revilers, nor extortioners, shall inherit the kingdom of God. 1 Cor 6:9-10

My Journey Home

My journey home was a lonely one. It was dark and fearful. I walked down a road of **hopelessness** toward a hill of despair. Turned left through the forest of **death** and down into the valley of **depression.**

And when I thought I was almost there, when I thought victory was within my reach, I found myself at the corner of a street called **confusion**. When I looked up towards heaven, hoping to find answers, I found myself looking up at **doubt**. I stopped to take a rest and I could feel the abuse of my battered life. I came across a corner with a sign that said keep on going, and then, I got lost again and found myself standing still knee deep in **disappointment**.

I was so tired. I decided to lie down and even it was a **bed of sorrow**. When I awoke I saw a light at the end of the road. There stood a rugged cross and a whisper, a still small voice asking, "wilt thou be made whole?" I said yes Lord, and the voice said, "pick up thy bed and walk."

For thou have been REDEEMED
Welcome Home

.

Made in the USA
Las Vegas, NV
24 October 2021

32940092R00069